WHAT YOU SHOULD KNOW ABOUT DEPRESSION
AND HOW TO COPE...

Depression is not for sissies!

I was first inspired to write this book after witnessing a loved one suffering from depression, which was a terrifying experience. Fortunately it was only a temporary episode, but it motivated me to research prevention of depression so it will hopefully never happen again. As I see it, knowledge and prevention is the key to break this increasing growth of depression worldwide.

With my book I hope to make everyone understand depression better and most importantly to know that it is possible to overcome depression with the right help, and to have happy and healthy lives after depression.

Everyone with depression should know this:
It is **never** your fault and your depression **can** be treated!

I sincerely hope that my book will be beneficial to you and yours.

Pernille Lund

TABLE OF CONTENTS.

1.FACTS ABOUT DEPRESSION.

Whether you are reading this book because you deal with depression yourself or know someone who does, or perhaps you work with people who are depressed, I think it is important that you know the dry clinical facts about depression.

This way you will also know that if you are depressed, you are certainly not alone about it! As a matter of fact, depression is currently the number one disability in the US and the 2nd biggest cause of disability in the world after back pain. Meaning depression is more common than the combined totals of diabetes, cancer and AIDS.

Globally, more than 350 million people of all ages, incomes and nationalities suffer from depression. And each year more than 17 million Americans suffer from a depressive illness. It is estimated that 10% of Americans suffers from some type of clinical depression at any given time, and that 20% of all Americans will suffer a major depression in their life time. And if you multiply these numbers with 2 or perhaps even 3, you will have the number of adults in the U.S. who experience some kind of depressive symptoms, but are never diagnosed.

Depression may occur just one time during your life. However, many people usually experience multiple episodes of depression, especially if your depression has gone untreated or have not been treated correctly. An untreated depression can lead to severe emotional or physical problems, which is why we have to take depression seriously and get the correct help.

Depression is often talked about as something weak and there can be a stigma attached to depression. But coming out of a serious depression and through to the other side intact and alive may be the strongest and bravest thing one will ever do...

"Depression is the inability to construct a future" (Rollo May)

2. WHAT IS DEPRESSION EXACTLY?

Someone once described depression like "It feels like drowning except that you can see everyone around you breathing, but not you".

Depression is a serious mental disorder which left untreated can be destructive and dangerous. Depression will cause you to feel an overwhelming feeling of sadness, and it is much more than just a low mood.

Depression comes from your brain, and academically speaking, it means that the neurotransmitters in your brain are out of balance. This imbalance is associated with depressive symptoms. So depression will affect how you feel, how you think and how you behave and can lead to both emotional and physical problems.

Depression can be long-lasting or recurrent, and it is a most disabling condition that will most likely impair your ability to function at work, in school or just coping with daily life.

Even though depression can be reliably diagnosed and treated, depression often remains undiagnosed and can negatively affect other medical conditions like diabetes and heart disease. Some people hide their depression by using drugs and alcohol, making it even harder to diagnose.

If you suffer from depression or know of someone suffering from this condition, it is very important that they contact their physician and be diagnosed. If the depression is severe or even moderate, professional help may be needed, as severe untreated depression can lead to suicide as almost 400,000 Americans make suicide attempts every year.

Feeling sad or depressed happens to all of us. This sensation usually passes after a while. If a friend says, "I'm so depressed today" she may mean, she is feeling tired or discouraged or has had a hard day at work. You can probably cheer her up with a good joke or a nice dinner. But a clinical depressed person is not able to laugh, think or ignore her way out as the depression will disrupt her entire life, and usually require some sort of long-term treatment.

Statistically most people with depression benefit from some kind of treatment, supplement or medication. But even though the treatments are widely available and generally successful, many people with depression never seek treatment.

3. WHAT CAUSES DEPRESSION?

Depression is currently thought to be caused by a combination of triggers including genetic, biological, environmental and psychological factors.

One recent study suggests that the risk of depression starts in the womb, as children whose mothers were depressed during their pregnancy will have an increased risk of 1.3 times higher than normal of suffering from depression in adulthood.

Also we know now that untreated long-term stress often leads to depression.

Changes in a person's hormone balance may cause or trigger depression as well. Several conditions are known to cause hormonal changes that include thyroid problems and menopause.

Depression can also be triggered by life events such as the loss of someone close to you, trauma, losing your job, divorce or any long-term stressful situation.

Many chronically ill patients suffer from depression. Up to 25% of all cancer patients will also get depression, which can eventually decrease the patient's survival rate. Chronic pain and frequent migraines can lead to depression as well.

Long term poor sleep problems and insomnia also increases the risk of depression. When the brain doesn't get the time to replenish brain cells during sleep, the brain doesn't function as well, and this can be one of the many factors leading to depression.

Some people, particularly young people and women, are also likely to develop depression with seasonal change. Especially when going from summer to fall/winter.

Some newer studies show that people living in urban areas have a 39% higher risk of developing depression than people living in rural areas. Especially postpartum depression is much more frequent in big cities.

The reason for this is believed to be the low level of social support during and after pregnancy and/or the level of stress in urban areas and larger cities being much higher than in more rural regions. And as mentioned before stress very often leads to depression.

Previously it was commonly believed that depression was nothing more than an exaggerated reaction to life's many challenges. More recently it was then suggested that depression is nothing but a chemical imbalance. However, both these two theories are too naive. Depression should rather be described as psychological and biological disorder of the whole person – mind, body and spirit.

The biological cause of clinical depression is an ongoing study, and no one knows the exact combination of factors that cause depression or how one can be 100% certain to avoid it.

"Depression opens the door to beauty of some kind" (James Hillman)

4. DEPRESSION AND THE BRAIN.

What is really going on inside the brain when depressed? Why do our personalities change? Will the brain ever become normal again? As complex as the brain is, I will try to explain the process of the brain during depression below.

I can assure you that even with the changes inside your brain during depression, your brain is set up to heal itself as well as it possible can. If an area of the brain is suffering, there are very often other areas of the brain ready to take over for the injured area. Depending on the severity of a depression and if there are other factors as well, such as anxiety or posttraumatic stress disorder, it will take time for your brain to feel as it did before your depression. Perhaps your memory will suffer a little. Or perhaps you can't read for as long as you used to read. Or you are unable to focus for two hours on a movie. But know this is ok. You are not going crazy. Depression takes time to heal and your brain takes time to heal. And even when the depressive symptoms are over, you may still feel different than you did before. But after two years or so, most people will feel like themselves again.

The brain: The researchers studying clinical depression look at the many aspects of brain functions and find the structures of the limbic system and the function of neurotransmitters, to be of main interest when it comes to depression and the brain.

The Limbic System and depression

Clinical depression researchers have been especially interested in the limbic system. This area of the brain affected by depression is the amygdala, the thalamus, the cerebral cortex and the hippocampus.

The amygdala is associated with emotions such as pleasure, physical and sexual drives, sorrow and fear. Activity in the amygdala is found to be higher in a person clinically depressed.

The hippocampus is associated with memory and recollection. The hippocampus is smaller in some depressed people, and some research suggests that ongoing exposure to stress impairs the growth of nerve cells (neurons) in this part of the brain.

The thalamus is associated with most sensory information. Some research shows that bipolar disorders may result from problems in the thalamus.

Limbic activities are so important and so sensitive, that any disturbance, including how the neurotransmitters function, can affect your mood and behavior.

Neurotransmitters and Neurons

Different depression research focus is on the function of neurons and neurotransmitters. In depressed brains, the neurotransmitters are not balanced, and this imbalance may be responsible for the depressive symptoms.

Chemicals called neurotransmitters carry out many important functions in the brain, such as transferring messages throughout structures of the brain's nerve cells. These nerve cells are called neurons. Each of us has up to 100 billion neurons in our brain. When we do anything, react, feel emotions or think, our neurons transmit messages in the form of electrical impulses. The electrical impulses change to chemical impulses, called a neurotransmitter, which will carry a message from one neuron to another.

Of the approximate 30 neurotransmitters that have been identified, researchers have discovered links between clinical depression and three primary neurotransmitters: serotonin, norepinephrine and dopamine. These three neurotransmitters function again in the structures of the brain regulating emotions, reactions to stress and the physical drives of sleep, appetite and sexuality.

Some studies show that antidepressant medications are effective because they regulate the amount of specific neurotransmitters in the brain. There appears to be a strong relationship between neurotransmitter levels in the brain and clinical depression.

Scientists are not certain whether changes in levels of neurotransmitters cause the development of depression, or if depression causes the changes in neurotransmitters. Researchers believe that our behavior can affect our brain chemistry, and that brain chemistry can affect behavior. For example if a person experiences much stress this could cause his or her brain chemistry to be affected and lead to clinical depression.

But what if the same person learned how to change depressed thoughts and behavior and cope with stressful events? Doing this may also change brain chemistry and relieve depression.

Hormones and the Endocrine System

Researchers searching for the causes of clinical depression also focus on the endocrine system. This system works with the brain to control many body activities. The endocrine system keeps the hormone levels from becoming too high through a feedback process, similar to a thermostat. If a hormone raises to a particular level the gland stops producing and releasing the hormone. When a person is depressed this feedback process may not function adequately. Problems with hormone levels may be connected to the change in brain chemistry seen in clinical depression.

The endocrine system is made of small glands that create hormones and release them into the blood. The hormones released by the glands regulate reaction to stress and sexual development. Many depressed people have abnormal levels of some hormones in their blood, even though their glands are healthy. Such hormonal irregularities may be connected to some depressive symptoms like problems with appetite and sleeping. Another clue to this connection is that sometimes people with certain endocrine disorders also develop depression, and some depressed people develop endocrine problems even though they have healthy glands.

Cortisol

Approximately 50% of clinical depressed persons, have an excess of the hormone cortisol in their blood. Cortisol is often named the harmful stress hormone. Cortisol is secreted by the adrenal glands. The adrenal glands help us react to stressful events. Cortisol may continue to be secreted even though the person already has high levels in his or her blood. Researchers believe cortisol is related to clinical depression because the high levels usually go back down to normal levels, when the depression disappears.

Some research has shown that the timing of the release of cortisol may be a problem for depressed persons. People who are not depressed tend to have secretions of cortisol at certain times of the day. Cortisol levels are highest in the morning and mid-afternoon and lowest during the night. This normal cycling of cortisol levels does not occur in some people, who are depressed. A depressed person may have a consistent high level of cortisol all the time, or have the highest amounts in the middle of the night.

Cortisol levels can be tested using a dexamethasone suppression test (DST). This is not a depression test, because some depressed people may not be identified by the test result. But the test can indicate abnormal levels of cortisol and further action can be taken from there to determine if a person is clinical depressed, severely stressed or have some other health issues.

Brain imaging can detect the biological differences in a depressed person's brain. Magnetic resonance imaging (MRI) has demonstrated that the brains of depressed people look different than the brains of non-depressed people. The difference in appearance can be seen in the parts of the brain involved in sleep, mood, appetite, thinking, learning and behavior.

Below are two pictures of two brains. The first one is showing a depressed person's brain and the other one is a picture of a depression free brain.

Notice the obvious different activity levels in the two brains.

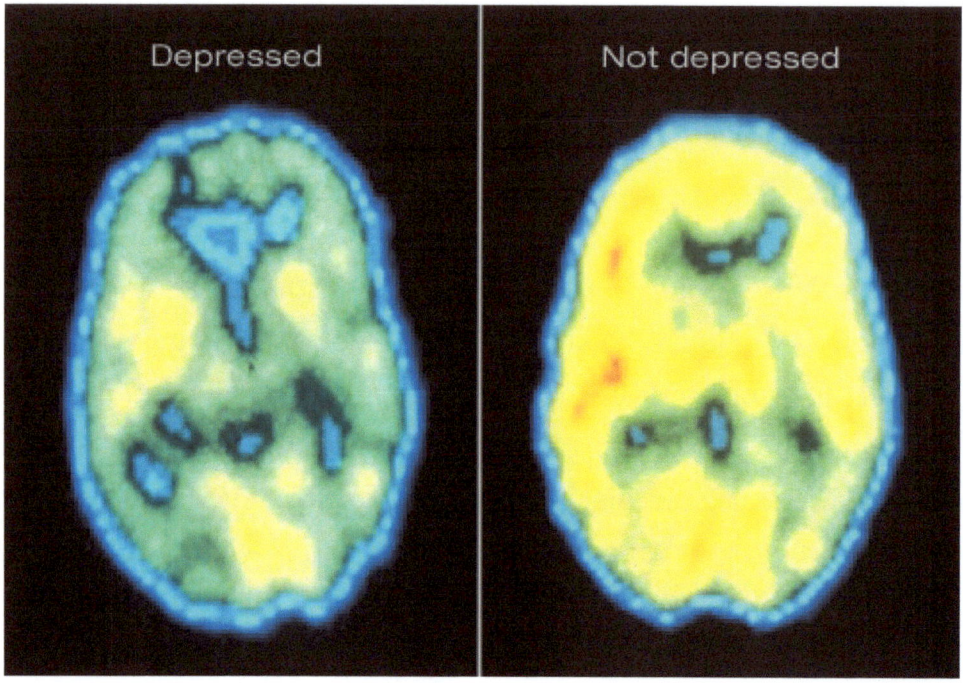

Most MRI studies made shows that depressed patients usually have an abnormal activation of the prefrontal cortex. With such clear images of a depressed brain versus a healthy brain, many physicians and researchers believe that in order to improve the efficiency of depression treatment and reduce the increase in depressive disorders, depression needs to be defined at the neurobiological level.

"Depression is an illness and not a necessary part of healthy living"
(David D. Burns)

5. ARE SOME PEOPLE MORE LIKELY TO GET DEPRESSED THAN OTHERS?

Perhaps you are afraid, that you may be doomed to get depressions since you have family members suffering from depression? As there is a slighter higher risk of you getting depressions as well, also remember that your family members perhaps did not know how to cope with certain life situations very well and therefore suffered depression. The fact that you are reading this book right now and learning about depression and how to cope is the first step to avoid getting depressed in the first place.

So yes, individuals with a family history of depression have a higher risk of developing depression themselves, than individuals without a family history. Researchers have found that for those suffering from depression, roughly 50 percent of the cause is genetic and the rest is the result of psychological and/or physical factors.

If your family has a depression history, what you inherit is a vulnerability to depression. This means that you inherit a tendency to develop the disorder. But it does not mean that you are destined to become depressed.

For example, if you have a parent or a sibling suffering from depression, you may be 1.5 to 3 times more likely to develop depression than people, who do not have a close relative with depression.

In general depression and other mental disorders, have a genetic component. This means that bipolar disorders (a manic-depressive illness) also have genetic connections. About 50% of people with bipolar disorders have a parent with a clinical depression history.

A recent study suggests that depressions could especially be linked to your mother, but this claim is still undergoing more research.

There have been many studies of identical twins and depression, and they have been the key to discovering information about genetics and depression.

Identical twins have the same genetic code. When one identical twin becomes depressed, the other will also develop clinical depression 76% of the time. If the identical twins are raised separated from each other, they will both become depressed about 67% of the time.

However, because the rate of both identical twins developing depression is not 100%, we know there are other contributing factors.

A person's vulnerability to depression is also influenced by childhood experiences, traumatic events, current stressors, exposure to substances, environmental factors and medical illnesses.

Fraternal twins share only about 50% of their genetic makeup with each other. When researchers studied these twins, they found that when one fraternal twin becomes depressed, the other also becomes depressed about 19% of the time. This is a higher rate of depression than the rate for the general public, and this supports the theory of genetic influence in the development of clinical depression.

Internationally, twice as many women as men are diagnosed with depression. However, that does not mean that men aren't susceptible to depression.
In fact, many researchers believe that men are equally vulnerable to the illness, but are less likely to seek treatment, because they fear it would be emasculating. Men with depression often exhibit different behavior than women. Men can have less emotional symptoms and act out with aggression instead or use alcohol or other substances. This behavior masks the illness and makes depression less likely to be identified in men than in women.

"Trust me, you know when you've got depression" (Giles Andreae)

6. WHAT DOES DEPRESSION FEEL LIKE

Do you think that you may have a depression, but is not sure? Below you can find information about the most common symptoms of depression but trying to diagnose yourself is never a good idea. If you believe you may have a depression, always go and see your physician and describe your symptoms as these can be parallel to other diseases. And if you do have depression it is advisable to discuss with your doctor which treatment route to take. Remember that depression is serious matter and if left untreated or if ignoring the symptoms it can worsen.

Depression can range from mild, temporary episodes of sadness to severe, persistent and overwhelming depression. A client described her depression as an immense state of sadness, darkness and inability to focus on even the slightest chores.

Clinical depression will affect how a person feels, behaves and thinks.

The depressive symptoms vary from person to person. Some symptoms will be felt by one person but no by another. The symptoms can occur most of the day, every day or almost every day. Some people have depression symptoms that are so severe, that anyone will notice something is wrong. Others with milder symptoms may just feel generally miserable or unhappy, and don't know why.

The most common symptoms of depression are:
A constant feeling of sadness
Emptiness and hopelessness
Anxiety
No energy, disturbed sleep patterns
Change of eating habits
Restlessness
No interest in activities and hobbies once enjoyed
Low sex drive
Difficulty in focusing and remembering details
Feelings of self-hatred

Feelings of guilt and blame
Feeling like crying
Persistent doubting and worrying
Anger
Irritability
Underperforming at work or in school
Avoiding social contact
Slow body movements and speech may be slower
Finding it impossible to enjoy life
Takes extra efforts to do small tasks
Frequent thoughts of death or suicidal thoughts

Physical symptoms may include: headaches, digestive problems, frequent body pain and change in women's menstrual cycle.

For major depression your symptoms must be so severe that they cause problems in relationships or in daily activities. Symptoms can be based on your own feelings or on someone else's observation.

Children and teens have similar depression symptoms as adults. In young children, depression symptoms can include being very clingy, irritable, sadness, introvert or underweight. Other symptoms include refusing to go to school, worrying, sleeping poorly and complaining of aches and pains. In teens, depression symptoms can include sudden sensitivity, feeling misunderstood, sadness, irritability, anger, poor school attendance, negative and worthless feelings, drug or alcohol abuse, self-harm, eating or sleeping too much, loss of interest and avoiding social interaction.

Other mental health issues can occur with depression. These include disorders, attention deficit/hyperactivity disorder (ADHD), anxiety, OCD and substance abuse.

Depression is not an age-related illness, and because older adults are often reluctant to seek help, depression often goes undiagnosed and untreated in this age group.

Depression symptoms in older adults may be slightly different or less obvious, including memory issues, personality changes, fatigue, appetite loss, wanting to stay at home in familiar surroundings, less social and not wanting to socialize or try new things, thoughts of suicide (especially in older men).

The Hamilton Depression Rating Scale (HAM-D) has proven useful for many years as a way to determine if a patient is depressed and also to monitor the depressed patient during and after treatment. It should always be monitored by a physician or a clinician experienced in working with psychiatric patients.

You can take a look at this widely used depression test on:

healthnet.umassmed.edu/mhealth/HAMD.pdf

It will give you an idea of important questions when determining depression, but please note that this test was not designed to be self-administered.

7. DIFFERENT TYPES OF DEPRESSION.

There are several types of depression:

The major depression has multiple symptoms that interfere with your ability to work, sleep, study, eat and enjoy activities. Major depression can prevent you from being totally functional. This depression may occur as a single episode but more often it occurs as multiple episodes throughout life. A major depression can last anywhere from 2 weeks to more than 2 years with the average length of an episode of depression being 6-8 months.

Dysthymic disorder, or dysthymia, or also referred to as mild chronic depression. Dysthymia patients have symptoms for 2 years or longer that may not be severe as in a major depression, and not severe enough to disable them, but can still prevent them from functioning normally or feeling well. People with dysthymia may also experience one or more episodes of major depression during their lifetime.

Minor depression creates 2-4 depressive symptoms for 2 weeks or longer that are not triggered by any events or stressors and don't quite meet the criteria for major depression. However unless they seek and receive treatment, people with minor depression are at high risk for developing major depression.

Postpartum depression, also known as **Post natal depression (PND),** is much more serious than the post-birth "baby blues" many women experience. It is estimated that 10-15% of women experience postpartum depression after giving birth, but sadly many go undiagnosed for long periods without help or support, causing problems between the mother and her newborn, trauma or severe sadness. Postpartum depression does not necessarily happen immediately after giving birth, but can occur up to a year after giving birth.

Seasonal affective disorder (SAD) is the onset of depression during the winter months, when there is less natural sunlight. This depression most often develops in the months between September and November and will continue until March or April. When the sunlight returns in spring or summer, the depression usually lifts. SAD may be effectively treated with light therapy, but half of the SAD patients don't get better with light therapy alone and need other treatment. Psychotherapy combined with light therapy has shown to be a good combination to reduce SAD symptoms.

Bipolar disorder is also called manic-depressive illness. It is not as common as major depression or dysthymia. A person with bipolar disorder experiences changing moods, from extreme highs (e.g. mania) to extreme lows (e.g. depression). These extremes are also called manias. Treatment tends to include mood stabilizing medications such as Lithium.

Psychotic depression is a combination of severe depression with a form of psychosis. Psychosis can include having delusions or hearing or seeing upsetting things often called hallucinations. Psychotic depression is also referred to as delusional depression. Psychotic depression affects about one out of every four patients admitted to the hospital for depression. Treatment is usually a combination of antidepressants and antipsychotic medications and is very effective with recovery normally within one year. Continual medical follow-up may be necessary though.

"Grief comes and goes, but depression is unremitting"
(Kay Redfield Jamison)

8. MYTHS ABOUT DEPRESSION.

There have always been myths about depression, and most people have an opinion of depression and what it is, who gets it and why. Here are some of the most common depression myths and the truth behind these misconceptions:

Myth: Depression is not a real medical illness
Truth: Clinical depression is indeed a serious medical condition that can affect your personality and you whole life. It affects your thoughts, your mood, your body and your ability to function normally. Depression is not a condition that you think yourself into. It has genetic, psychological and biological causes. Everyone coping with depression has higher level of stress hormones in their bodies and MRI brain scans of depressed people will show decreased and altered activity in some areas of the brain.

Myth: Depression is no different from getting "the blues" and this is just a normal part of life
Truth: The blues are something that most people experience at some point in their life. Disappointments, ordinary sadness and minor setbacks can make you feel down, glum or have "the blues", but it usually only lasts for a short while. However, no one commits suicide because they have the blues. Depression is an illness that can overwhelm and disable you. A depression does not disappear with time or by willpower. Depression can last a lifetime and requires immediate attention.

Myth: People with depressions are just feeling sorry for themselves
Truth: Depression affects up to 19 million people annually in the U.S. alone, and some of the individuals who have suffered from depression include Alexander the Great, Abraham Lincoln, Theodore Roosevelt, Winston Churchill, Napoleon Bonaparte, George Patton, Barbara Bush, Robert E. Lee, Florence Nightingale, Sir Isaac Newton, Charles Darwin, J.P. Morgan, Ludwig van Beethoven and Michelangelo. These are all people who didn't just sit around feeling sorry about themselves despite suffering from depression.

Myth: Depression only affects women

Truth: Statistically, women seek treatment for depression twice as often as men do, but this may not reflect the real rates of depression among men. Clinical depression is widely underreported by men. This may occur because of the stigma of depression, and the substance abuse that can disguise depression. It is very important to urge men with depression symptoms to seek help, because men have a higher rate of successful suicide attempts than women.

Myth: Even if depression is a medical illness, there is nothing that can be done about it

Truth: More than 80 percent of people with depression improve with treatment. As new treatments, supplements and medications are discovered, this number will probably continue to rise. If you are experiencing the symptoms of depression, first have a doctor test you and confirm that these symptoms are not caused by another condition like thyroid problems or stress. If you are diagnosed with depression, work with your doctor to start treatment, whether it includes psychotherapy, counseling, medication, a weekly talk with your doctor to monitor your symptoms, or a combination of all the options available. However, it is important to know that treatment for depression takes time, and full recovery can take many months or even years.

Myth: Depression will go away by itself

Truth: Some depressed people may experience the depression lifting by itself. But that is the exception. Depression can hang on indefinitely and depression symptoms rarely go away if untreated. Clinical depression can be a potentially fatal disease if you wait around for it to resolve itself. Seek help now if you are experiencing the symptoms of depression.

Myth: Depression means I am weak

Truth: Being depressed does not mean you are weak or mentally unsound! Depression can strike anyone and at anytime, no matter how strong we are as it knows no bounds. Some people believe that if you are strong enough, you can just think the depression away, but depression is also a very physical illness, and cannot be dismissed like a pesky thought. It is caused by chemical changes in the brain. Know that by seeking help for your depression you are being strong, and never weak. Actually some of the strongest people in history have suffered from depression throughout their lives.

Myth: Depression is a normal part of aging
Truth: Depression is not a normal part of the aging process and depression occurs in all age groups. But seniors often experience more events that can trigger depressions such as loss of family members, poor health, isolation and financial anxiety. Some seniors may feel embarrassed to ask for help. The highest rate of suicide of any group occurs in people 65 and older. Men are more vulnerable than women. If you are, or know, a senior with depression, take action and seek help for them. Whether you are 65 or 85, nobody has to live with depression. Senior depression can be treated and with the right help and support, seniors can live happy, active and vibrant lives.

Myth: Children and teenagers do not get depression. Their problems and behavior are just a part of growing up
Truth: The National Institute of Mental Health reports that 1 in 33 children and 1 in 8 adolescents are depressed in any one year. It is important for adults to become familiar with the symptoms of depression in young people and be pro-active in helping them to get assistance from a professional.

Myth: If a close family member suffers from depression, you will also suffer from it
Truth: If there is depression in your biological family, it can increase your risk of becoming depressed by approximately 10-15%. However, it does not guarantee that you will also get it. Statistically, your risk of getting a depression is higher than if you had no family history of this illness, but studies show that there are several interactive factors besides genetics that can trigger depression.

"Depression is a flaw in chemistry, not in character"

9. IS DEPRESSION DANGEROUS?

Yes!
Untreated depression can result in emotional, behavioral and health problems that affect every area of your life, and untreated depression can have serious consequences.

Complications associated with depression may include following:
Panic disorder, anxiety and/or social phobia
Alcohol or substance abuse
Social isolation
Reckless behavior
Family conflicts, relationship difficulties, and work or school problems
Excess weight that can lead to heart disease and diabetes
Thoughts of suicide, suicide attempts, or suicide
Self-mutilation, including cutting and burning
Premature death from other medical conditions

Depression often co-exists with other illnesses. These co-occurring illnesses also need to be diagnosed and treated.
Some common examples of these illnesses are:
Anxiety disorders, like post-traumatic stress disorder (PTSD), obsessive-compulsive disorder (OCD), panic disorder, social phobia and generalized anxiety disorder.

It is very common for people with PTSD to have co-existing depression.
PTSD can occur after a person experiences a terrifying event or ordeal such as a violent assault, a natural disaster, an accident, terrorism or military combat. These can all trigger PTSD.

In a study funded by the National Institute of Mental Health (NIMH), researchers found that more than 40 percent of people with PTSD also had depression 4 months after the traumatic event.

Alcohol and other substance abuse or dependence may also co-exist with depression as research shows that mood disorders and substance abuse commonly occur together. Depression may also occur with other serious medical illnesses such as heart disease, stroke, cancer, HIV/AIDS, diabetes and Parkinson's disease.

People who have depression along with another medical illness tend to have more severe symptoms of both depression and the medical illness, more difficulty adapting to their medical condition and more medical costs than those, who do not have co-existing depression. One example is heart patients. Studies show that depression can make heart disease worse, and make it more difficult to recover from complications of heart disease. Depression can also increase your risk of having a heart attack. And having a depression increases your risk of dying by nearly 20% in the first 6 months after a heart attack. Treating the depression may also help improve the outcome of treating the co-occurring illness.

Long term depression may also contribute to loss of brain power, especially in elderly patients, and frequent untreated depressions early in life may contribute to the development of Alzheimer's disease, strokes and senility.

So after reading the above you now know that depression is indeed serious.
And if you are feeling depressed you should make a doctor's appointment today.

Depression most often gets worse if untreated. And depression can lead to other mental and physical health problems or troubles in other areas of your life as well as the most serious depression can inflict serious or fatal self-harm.

**"Grief is depression in proportion to circumstance and
Depression is grief out of proportion to circumstance"
Andrew Solomon**

10. WHAT ARE SOME OF THE NATURAL COPING STRATEGIES FOR DEPRESSION?

If you are suffering from depression, there are many different things you can do to feel better. Some coping strategies will not appeal to you, and some you will enjoy, and they will make you feel better little by little. I know when you are depressed, you do not have the energy to do much or take on any new tasks. And that is ok. But try to implement little coping strategies into your life, step by step. I promise you, that you will feel better when you do.

Here are some tips that have been shown to be effective:

First seek help, get diagnosed and talk with a professional about your symptoms and your feelings.

Locate helpful organizations for advice. The National Alliance on Mental Illness (NAMI) and the Depression and Bipolar Support Alliance (DBSA) offer education, support groups, counseling and other resources to help with depression. Some employee assistance programs and churches also offer help for mental health concerns.

Keep your life simple. Cut back on your obligations and set reasonable goals for yourself. Permit yourself to do less, or nothing, when you feel down.

Keep a journal. Journaling can improve your mood because it allows you to express pain, sorrow, anger, fear or other emotions. Also end your day every day by journaling 3-5 positive things that happened in your life that day. There are always some good things, even the smallest thing to feel grateful about. It can be something simple as nice weather, a good rest, a nice email, birds singing etc. Know that it is virtually impossible to feel grateful and to feel sad at the same time. So focus on the positive, even on days when it seems impossible.

Do not let yourself become isolated. Reach out. Get or stay involved in your community. Participate in social activities and get together with friends and family regularly, even on the days when you don't feel up to it. Seeing loved ones will help you feel better, and if you are very low on energy, you can just cut the visit short. People will understand if you explain the situation. Staying home will perpetuate the depression. Make an agreement with a friend who enjoys talking on the phone frequently to speak every day or every other day. Even if just for five minutes. A conversation helps to break the feelings of isolation.

Read widely recognized self-help books and websites. But be selective and read the most reputable sources on depression help.

Structure your time. Plan your day. Get up at the same time every day. Eat meals at the same time. Make a daily to-do list. Set small simple goals every day. Use a planner to stay organized. Check off items as you accomplish them to enjoy your productivity. This will give you a sense of normality that can help ease a depressed mood.

Stop ruminating. Rumination is obsessive thinking about a problem, amplifying the stress, the anger and anxiety associated with the memory. This type of thinking is linked to a greater risk at becoming or staying depressed, and is shown to be very damaging to mental health. If you catch yourself ruminating, try to distract yourself with a healthy activity instead, meditate and redirect your thoughts.

Do not make important decisions when you are down. Avoid making big and life changing decisions when you are feeling depressed, since you may not be thinking clearly. Wait until you feel better and stronger.

Be mindful – stay in the present. Try not to worry about the future or dwell with the past. Worrying about the future or the past is adding to your depressive thoughts.

Eat a healthy diet, drink water, go for a walk every day (even if it just for 10 minutes) as the sunlight and fresh air will do you good and remember to get plenty of sleep.

Take good care of yourself and treat yourself nicely. Think about inner dialogue with yourself and keep it positive. Do not beat yourself up because you are depressed and cannot manage your daily tasks. Be your own best friend, and treat yourself as well as you treat your best friends.

Think about this period of your life as a time where it is ok to nurture yourself and to be selfish, putting yourself and your health and wellbeing first.

Try to have fun. Watch your favorite fun TV show, make time for things that you enjoy and try to have a good laugh every day. You may not find anything funny right now, which is a normal depression symptom, but try anyway.

Help someone else by volunteering.

Care for a pet if possible. Pets can bring joy and companionship into your life, and help you feel less isolated. At the same time caring for a pet will also give you a sense of being needed which is an important feeling when depressed.

Learn techniques to relax and manage any stress. Techniques could include meditation, progressive muscle relaxation, yoga, tai chi and qigong. Look for relaxing hobbies you truly enjoy (must not feel like a burden) such as gardening, cooking, music, painting, reading and daily walks.

"Depression and I are old friends, but I do not court his company"
(Laura K Rhodes)

"The greatest degree of inner tranquility comes from the development of love and compassion. The more we care for the happiness of others, the greater is our own sense of well-being"

Tenzin Gyatso

11. IS IT POSSIBLE TO OVERCOME DEPRESSION WITHOUT MEDICATION?

Certainly, there are many people who have suffered with depression who are now symptom-free without taking anti-depressive medication. There does not appear to be an identical roadmap for every depressed person to take to achieve wellness from depression. However, sometimes you must try different methods before finding the right one for your depression. Believe that one of the many anti-depressive methods available and which you pursue will ultimately work, whether it will be a chemical anti-depressants or a more natural way.

Most physicians will recommend a mix of medication and psychotherapy as this have shown to be a successful treatment for many.

But if you are not prone to medication speak with your doctor about this and if he or she thinks it is safe then you can perhaps begin with psychotherapy and some of the other treatment methods. But know that this is also a matter of how severe the depression is, and that your depression is best monitored by a mental health professional.

When it comes to psychotherapy there are 3 options:

Cognitive behavioral therapy (CBT)
Interpersonal therapy
Psychodynamic therapy

There is really no simple answer to which works best as it is very individual and sometimes we have to try out different options to find the right one and not just settle for the first one available. Many people will find that a mix of elements from the different schools of psychotherapy suits them best, but again, it is very individual. However when it comes to gender, most research find that men and women benefit equally well from psychotherapy.

Psychotherapy is also known as talk therapy, counseling or psychosocial therapy.

The duration of psychotherapy for depression can be anywhere from 2 months to more than 2 years, depending on the severity and underlying issues of the depression. And group, family or couple therapy may also be part of a plan to treat depression.

A mental health professional will diagnose the depression either as a chronic or as an episodic depression, and since chronic depression lasts longer and is generally more severe than episodic depression, treatment is also more intensive. Relapsing is a major concern as about half of the people suffering from chronic depression will suffer a relapse if they stop treatment. And for that reason, an ongoing type of therapy treatment may be necessary.

Studies have shown that rumination, or replaying the same thoughts over and over in your head, plays an important role in depression. Rumination, insomnia and depression are now believed to be interconnected. This type of rumination is commonly found among those with depression or anxiety issues. Thinking repetitive negative thoughts actually is thought to encourage depression.

Psychological counseling (Psychotherapy) is an effective treatment for many depressed people with repetitive thoughts. It treats depression by encouraging you to talk about your condition and related underlying issues with a mental health provider.

Mindfulness-based cognitive therapy is advisable for people who are currently well, but have had 3 or more episodes of depression. This therapy is also a talking treatment and there is very good evidence that it can help prevent the recurrence of depression.

There are some severely depressed patients who do not improve with medication, psychotherapy and any other therapeutic assistance, and they may benefit from ECT (Electroconvulsive therapy), but this treatment is always considered as a last resort. ECT can sometimes be beneficial for treatment resistant depression, when everything else have been tried, and especially if patients are considered to be in danger of self-harm. ECT – formerly known as shock therapy has improved greatly over the years, and has helped improve severe depressions in some patients. The side effects can be confusion, memory loss and disorientation, but they tend to disappear not too long after the ECT treatment is finished.

It is important for anyone depressed to understand, that depression generally is not a disorder that you can treat on your own. So it is best advised not to skip talk therapy sessions. And even if not feeling well, do not skip you medications either. If you stop the medication your depression symptoms may come back and you could also experience withdrawal symptoms. Always speak to your physician about stopping a prescribed medication and how to do it.

If you are depressed, learning about depression is important, as the knowledge will empower you and motivate you to stick to your treatment plan as well as help prevent you getting more depressions in the future.

Pay attention to the warning signs. Work with your doctor or therapist to learn what triggers your depression. Plan what to do if your symptoms get worse. Ask friends to help you watch for warning signs.

Exercise whenever you have the strength to do it. Physical activity reduces depression symptoms. Consider walking, jogging, swimming, biking, gardening or pursuing any other activity that you enjoy. Intimacy is also great for reducing stress and depression symptoms.

Avoid alcohol and illegal drugs. In the long run, alcohol and illegal drugs generally worsen symptoms and make the depression harder to treat. Talk with your doctor or therapist if you need help with alcohol or substance abuse.

Alternative medicine for depression is another popular option for patients who are not keen on medication in general. It is important to understand that there are risks as well as possible benefits of alternative or complementary therapy and supplements. Don't replace your conventional medical treatment or psychotherapy with these suggestions without talking to your mental health professional first.

Alternative treatments are not always a suitable substitute for medical care.

Also you must know that nutritional and dietary products are not monitored by the FDA like prescription medications are. You can't always be certain what you are getting, and if it is safe. Also, because some herbal and dietary supplements can interfere with prescription medications or cause dangerous interactions, talk to your health care provider before taking any supplements, as he/she may have some reliable experience with the supplements you want to try.

Examples of herbal remedies and supplements that are sometimes or often used for depression include:

St. John's Wort is a herb which is not (yet) approved by the FDA to treat depression in the United States, but it is a very popular depression treatment many places in Europe. Some studies show that it may help you, if you have a mild to moderate depression. Studies show a good effect with about 50% of patients benefitting from St. John's Wort, and if combined with another herb, Valerian, up to 68% of patients felt improvement in their depression. There are also seemingly good results with St. John's Wort for patients with stress, anxiety as well as headaches.
However, St. John's Wort should be used cautiously as it can interfere with antidepressants, HIV/AIDS medications and drugs to prevent organ rejection after an organ transplant, with birth control pills, blood-thinning medications and chemotherapy drugs. Also the effect on bipolar depression and psychotic/delusional depression are still rather unknown. So be sure to speak to your doctor if you consider taking this supplement and be sure to purchase only from a reliable supplier.

SAMe is a dietary supplement and the name is short for S-Adenosylmethionine. It is actually a synthetic form of a chemical, an amino acid, which the body produces naturally. SAMe helps produce and break down brain chemicals, such as serotonin, melatonin and dopamine. Researchers are not quite sure, why SAMe have such a good effect on depression, but think it may increase the amount of serotonin in our brain, similar to some antidepressants. Just like St. John's Wort, SAMe is not approved by the FDA to treat depression in the United States, but it is widely used in

Europe as a prescription drug to treat depression, and studies show, that this supplement can help stabilize mood. SAMe reportedly works very fast compared to prescribed drugs, and relieves depression symptoms in a couple of weeks, where traditional antidepressants usually take about 4-8 weeks to relieve symptoms. SAMe has also shown beneficial to other depression related conditions. No adverse effects have generally been reported in studies but some studies of SAMe have shown that while it often energizes patients with bipolar, it may also have the ability to trigger mania in bipolar patients, so more research is needed. Also it should not be taken without consulting with your doctor beforehand, as it can conflict with other medications. Especially medication for diabetes, antidepressants and medication for Parkinson's disease can be an issue combined with SAMe.
SAMe is also a rather expensive supplement, but you can enhance your body's own production of it by getting more B12 and folate in your diet.

5-HTP (5-HYDROXYTRYPTOPHAN) is also fast becoming a popular anti-depressant relief. 5-HTP is the chemical that your body makes from the amino acid, Tryptophan, which is then changed into serotonin. 5-HTP is not found in the foods that we eat so supplements are made from the seeds of an African plant "Griffonia Simplicifolia". Some studies indicate that 5-HTP works as well as the antidepressants drugs used to treat mild to moderate depressions, and with fewer side effects. 5-HTP is also showing good results for insomnia as well as chronic pain and migraine headaches. But while there are many positive recommendations on the internet for 5-HTP further studies are needed. High doses of 5-HTP have shown toxic issues, such as liver and brain toxicity, so in general you should see your doctor before taking 5-HTP to determine the correct dose for you.

The 2 Omega-3 fatty supplements DHA and EPA are being studied as a possible treatment for depression as it seems they may play an essential role in stabilizing mood.
These healthy fats are found naturally in cold-water fish, flaxseed, flax oil, walnuts and other foods. While considered generally safe, high doses of Omega-3 supplements may interact with medications. More research is needed to determine if eating foods with Omega-3 fatty acids can help relieve depression, but researchers are actually very optimistic about the positive effect Omega-3 has on different brain

functions, as well as a mood enhancer. A daily dose of 200 grams is recommended. Some people avoid eating fish due to worries about mercury and toxins. However, most experts agree that the benefits of eating 2 servings a week of fatty cold-water fish far outweigh the risks.

Rhodiola Rosea, commonly known as "rose root" is a popular depression relief supplement especially in Scandinavia and Russia. It is a plant which grows in high altitudes such as Siberia, and is one of the few plants which can grow in freezing temperatures. Researchers from Columbia University College found that Rhodiola Rosea improved mood, better sleep, increased energy, enhanced cognitive function, sexual function and both mental and physical performance during stress. Two dose levels were found to significantly reduce depression symptoms in patients with mild to moderate depression. There are many other studies to validate effectiveness Rhodiola Rosea and no significant negative effects. It is important to follow the recommended doses though, as taking too much Rhodiola Rosea can make some people feel jittery or agitated. Also it is recommended to be taken early in the day, before noon, as it can interfere with sleep.

In holistic thinking the mind-body connection is generally considered very important and complementary and alternative medicine practitioners believe that the mind and body must be in harmony for you to stay healthy.

Examples of mind-body techniques that may be helpful for depression include: music or art therapy, reflexology, acupuncture, meditation, yoga, Reiki healing, massage therapy, guided imagery, relaxation techniques, praying and spirituality. These therapies may be helpful when used in addition to professional treatment for depression.

12. DEPRESSION AND SLEEP.

You cannot sleep your way out of a depression, but we know by now that getting plenty of sleep, and especially when depressed, is a necessity. But unfortunately sleeping poorly is a frequent complaint from many depression patients. If you had sleep issues before your depression it may turn into chronic insomnia, which can be very difficult from which to break free. The relationship between sleep and depression is complex. Depression may cause sleep problems – and sleep problems may contribute to depressive disorders.

It is important to address sleep problems to recover from depression. Very often a physician will prescribe a sleep medication for insomnia but this is a very habit forming medication which also holds side effects, and should be used cautiously.

However, there is a recent study out which has shown, that ending your insomnia could be a big step toward breaking out of depression, so it is definitely well worth working on your sleep problems and try to stabilize them.

The National Institute of Mental Health (NIMH) recently released a new report on sleep and depression. It stated that more than half of the people with depression also suffer from insomnia. And it found, that curing insomnia may actually double your ability to fully recover from depression. The study was conducted by Ryerson University, where they studied 66 patients over a treatment period of 8 weeks. Instead of sleep medication, they used talk therapy to resolve the patient's insomnia.

The results confirmed findings of a pilot study:

1. 87% of those who were relieved of their insomnia through bi-weekly talk therapy sessions, also resolved their depression.
2. Participants who were unable to relieve their insomnia were only half as likely to resolve their depression.

The participants were introduced to talk therapy, talking about their emotions, sleep issues and behaviors that may have impeded their sleep. Then they were taught a technique called cognitive behavior therapy for insomnia (CBT-I).

Dr. Colleen Carney, the author if the study, said the objective is to "Curb this idea that sleeping requires effort, that it is something you have to fix...People get in trouble when they begin to think they have to do something to get to sleep"

CBT-I teaches patients to:
Get out of bed during waking periods
Avoid eating, reading, watching TV or similar activities in bed.
Establish a regular bedtime and wake-up time and stick to it.
Avoid napping.
Keep a sleep diary.
Use visualization and relaxation techniques.

All in all CBT-I has shown a very good success rate in decreasing insomnia and depression simultaneously, and with some marvelous advantages. First of all it is a very low cost and relatively fast treatment process. Also CBT-I does not involve prescription sleep aids with the side effects these can have.

This is the first result of many more sleep-depression studies, but if suffering from depression and insomnia, it is definitely worth looking into sleep-therapy and CBT-I therapy.

Good ways to cope with sleep problems are to:
Keep a regular sleep/wake schedule

Get into bright light soon after waking in the morning

Limit caffeine and alcohol

If you have nighttime insomnia, avoid taking naps during the day

Get some form of exercise during the day, but do not exercise in the evening

Practice a relaxing bedtime ritual such as a warm bath, meditating or listening to soft music and stay offline the last hour before bed.

If you suffer from insomnia or sleep issues and are not comfortable taking sleep medication, try to seek professional help from a sleep therapist.

13. DEPRESSION AND EXERCISE.

While it is doubtful, that we can purely exercise our way out of a serious depression with no other treatment, exercise is proven to help beat depression, and exercise is also one of the best ways to prevent depression happening in the first place.

Studies now show that the benefits of exercise are longer lasting than any other treatment for depression. Some studies also show that exercise alone works better than exercise with the most commonly used anti-depression medication, Selective Serotonin Reuptake Inhibitors (SSRIs).

Exercise prescription is now often the first choice treatment for clients who take many medications already. During moderate exercise, chemicals are released from the brain and participants may experience a heightened euphoric state called a "runner's high". This might explain some of the immediate benefits of exercise to counter depression. Over time, the effects of exercise may also help depressed people feel like they are taking control of their lives.

And the exercise does not have to be extensive or exhausting. A study showed that just walking approx. 35 minutes a day, 6 days a week, can decrease your level of depression by 47%! Exercising can seem challenging for a depressed person, especially if one is not used to exercising. However it is important to stress, that exercise does not mean running a marathon or long, tiring, intensive workouts.

Moderate exercise can also be a nice long walk with a friend or a dog or it can be dancing, swimming, gardening or even cleaning! Nothing strenuous about this, but it is still effective enough to help a depressed person feel better, if done for 30 minutes each day. And if 30 minutes seem unmanageable at first, then recommend dividing the 30 minutes into three 10- minute's exercise blocks a day. This is fine too, and gives the same benefits as one 30-minutes exercise period.

Now this next part may sound a little heavy and too scientific, but I included it, because it is from a new and important study about how exercise protects our brain and makes it more resilient from becoming stressed and depressed.

Humans and animals both gain valuable emotional benefits from exercise, as well as physical and mental benefits. In recent experiments with mice, scientists have traced the stress-buffering effect of exercise to a brain circuit involved in emotional regulation, mood disorders and medication effects. This may help us discover the neurological roots of resilience and could help science develop new ways to prevent and treat stress-related and depressive disorders.

National Institute of Mental Health scientists used a mouse model that mirrored the impact of social stress on mood in humans. Researchers demonstrated that mice that were housed in an environment with plenty of opportunities for exercise and exploration are unfazed by bullying.

These exercising mice were resilient compared to a second group of mice that were housed in a plain crowded environment. This second group of mice reacted to bullying in a passive and cautious way that suggested depression.

The benefits from activity and stimulation depend on the growth of new neurons in the brain in mice. The NIMH investigators carrying out this study then looked within the brain to see what exercise was actually changing inside the brain to protect the mice against stress.

They focused on a functional circuit of brain centers known to be involved in emotional processing. In mice that had been housed in an enriched environment, levels of a protein that signals the activity level of neurons were increased in cells in the infra limbic cortex (ILC), which is a part of this circuit. Parts of the brain closely wired to ILC showed elevated activity. Enrichment had the opposite effect on a part of the brain that is an important trigger for the body's stress response system.

So enrichment enhanced positive behavior and dampened activity in an area linked with an increased stress response.

The areas in the brain examined in this study are similar to brain regions with altered function in people with disorders like depression and post traumatic disorder.

Researchers don't exactly know yet why exercise is such a good antidepressant but evidence suggests that physical activity enhances new cell growth in the brain, increases mood-enhancing neurotransmitters and endorphins, relieves muscle tension and reduces stress – all good things which can have a positive effect on depression.

Exercising is also one of the main prevention strategies to becoming depressed in the first place, so there really isn't anything negative to be said about exercising and depression. And also knowing that there are no side effects to moderate exercise either, unlike medication, this could be the biggest motivator of all in the effort to beat depression.

14. DEPRESSION AND NUTRITION.

Can you eat your way out of a depression? No, probably not. No studies have been done that indicate a particular diet can ease the symptoms of a clinical depression. However, when you are depressed, you don't want to stress your body and brain even more by feeding it the wrong food and a healthy diet may help as part of an overall treatment for depression.

Depression will very often cause our eating habits to suffer. Some people will overeat turning to food for comfort. Others will lose their appetite and as a result feel even more depleted for energy. Others again are too tired to shop for and prepare nutritious meals and turn to fast food with little or no nutrition.

When you are depressed, it is important to listen to your body and to take good care of it. Nutrients in food support the body's repair, growth and wellness.

What you eat affects your mood and our mood affects which foods we want to eat. Some foods and beverages can negatively affect the way we feel.

Two mood-effecting substances commonly used are caffeine and sugar.
A helping of sugar gives you instant energy. But soon afterward your energy drops and you become sleepy. You may use caffeine to stay alert and productive.
But caffeine can also make you irritable, shaky, anxious, nauseous and headachy.
Many depressed people also have a craving for baked goods, but these feel-good foods quickly lead to a crash in mood and energy.

In comparison, healthy alternative foods can improve your mood without leaving you depleted hours later.

Choosing healthy and nutritious foods to assist boost your mood is a good anti-depressive strategy.

Some studies suggest Omega-3 fatty acids and Vitamin B12 enriched food are good choices, as they may ease mood changes that are part of depression.

Here are some basic guidelines to encourage you to follow a brain-healthy diet:

1) Increase your water intake. The human brain is 80% water. For brain nutrition you need to drink adequate water to hydrate your brain. Slight dehydration can raise stress hormones that can damage your brain. Try and drink at least 84 ounces of water a day.

2) DHA, one form of omega-3 fatty acids found in fish make up a big portion of your brain's grey matter. The fat in your brain form cell membranes and plays a central role in how our cells function. Neurons are also rich in omega-3 fatty acids and a diet rich in omega-3 fats may help promote a healthy emotional balance and positive mood as you age. If vegetarian, DHA is also available as a non-fish based supplement, made from the algae that the fish eat.

You can find omega-3 fatty acids in fish such as Salmon, Tuna, Herring, anchovies, sardines and Mackerel (When cooking fish it is better to bake, steam or grill rather than fry) Omega-3 fats are also found in flaxseed, tofu, nuts, soybeans and dark vegetables.

Vegetarians, who do not eat fish, can get omega-3 and vitamin B12 in supplements and in fortified cereals and dairy products.

3) Serotonin is a neurotransmitter that makes us feel good and happy. Between 80-90% of Serotonin is produced by cells in our guts, and not our brain. Serotonin was tied to food before it was tied to our moods. When your supply is low, you feel more depressed. When there's plenty of serotonin, we feel happier.
Studies show that supplementing with serotonin for a year, increased mood positively in women.

So our serotonin level is important, especially when we are depressed, and serotonin can be found in a variety of good foods, such as walnuts, tomatoes, kiwis, pineapples, plums and plantains.

4) Serotonin needs a helper to cross the blood-brain barrier in the brain and this helper is Tryptophan. Tryptophan is an amino acid key to serotonin production in our brains, when serotonin levels are low. Our bodies need for serotonin cause us to crave tryptophan, which is found in fish, eggs, beans, turkey, nuts, yogurt and milk.

5) A diet rich in protein is also a diet rich in the amino acid, Tyrosine. Tyrosine may help boost levels of the brain chemicals dopamine and norepinephrine. This will help you feel more alert and easier to focus, remember and concentrate. So when you need a boost in energy or to clear your mind, try to include a healthy and lean protein into your diet. Good sources of healthy protein are beans and peas, poultry, fish, lean beef, milk, soy products, yogurt and low-fat cheese.

6) It is also recommended to eat lots of dietary antioxidants.
According to some studies, eating antioxidants from fruits and vegetables can significantly reduce the risk of cognitive impairment.

According to the US Department of Agriculture the best antioxidant fruits and vegetables are:

Blueberries
Blackberries
Cranberries
Strawberries
Raspberries
Plums
Oranges
Red grapes
Cherries
Kiwis
Lemons
Limes
Grapefruit
Cantaloupe
Apricots

Peaches

Cauliflower

Carrots

Spinach

Brussels sprouts

Broccoli

Beets

Tomatoes

Avocados

Red or yellow bell peppers

Pumpkin

Squash

Eat the fruit fresh when in season, or frozen.

7) Recent research shows that a calorie-restricted diet helps your brain and your body live longer and cutting your risk of disease. It also triggers the production of nerve growth factors that help the brain stay strong. However, this is all new research and has to be studied further, and it is not suggested, that you can or should ever starve yourself out of a depression.

8) Prioritize to put the top healthy foods into your diet and try to stick to nutritional "brain healthy" foods as often as you possible can. The following foods are recommended daily or frequently, as they help you reach the goal of consuming antioxidants, lean protein, good fat and high fiber carbohydrates:

Oats, whole wheat, wheat germ

Yams

Beans

Lentils

Sweet potatoes

Extra virgin cold pressed olive oil

Coconut (also coconut oil)

Olives
Nut butter
Salmon, herring, mackerel
Nuts, especially walnuts, macadamia nuts, brazil nuts, pecans and almonds
Skinless chicken and turkey
Fish
Lean beef
Eggs
Tofu and soy products
Low fat cheeses, cottage cheese
Low fat yogurt
Low fat milk or skim milk

Bananas are considered by many a "brainy super-food" as it holds magnesium to decrease anxiety, tryptophan to boost the feel-good serotonin levels and vitamin 6 to promote alertness.

Brown rice contains serotonin as well as thiamine to support sociability.

And spinach is rich on magnesium plus folate to improve sleep and reduce agitation.

In general, it is always a good idea to choose whole foods and look for clean and uncontaminated food, and minimize processed food products as they typically contains ingredients not good for us, and which will only deplete our brain and bodies even further. However, when that is said, it is not suggested that you cannot eat ice cream, drink coffee or have pizza, when you are depressed. Of course you can. But think in balanced meals, so your body and brain will get everything they need while they are weak and not functioning optimally.

Getting better from depression demands a lifelong commitment and I have made that commitment for my life's sake and for the sake of those who love me.
(Susan Polis Schutz)

15. NEW STUDIES ABOUT DEPRESSION.

Studying depression and how to cope with depression in a healthy and non-harmful way is an ongoing study. Here are some results from newer studies that are rather interesting.

Can Probiotics Alter Your Depression?

If depressed, perhaps it's time to hit the yogurt?
You have probably heard that probiotics in yogurt, dietary supplements and natural food products can improve your digestive health and even boost your immune system. Now recent research suggests that some of the beneficial live bacteria may also offer a promising new way to treat depression.

The authors of a new review of studies from University College Cork in Ireland have found evidence that some probiotics offer untapped potential for the treatment of depression and other stress-related disorders.
The researchers cited one study that assessed the potential benefits of a specific probiotic, (B. Infantis) in rats that displayed depressive behavior. The probiotic treatment boosted the rat's immune response and returned them to normal behavior.
In another study cited by the researchers, healthy volunteers received either a probiotic combination or an inactive placebo for 30 days. Those who received the probiotics reported lower stress levels. In a related study, volunteers who consumed a daily yogurt containing probiotics generally reported improved mood.

The researchers strongly support the theory that some probiotics have the potential to exert behavioral, mental and immunological effects. Some psychobiotics have been proven to ease inflammation in the body as well, which has been tied to stress and depression.

The development of products that contain probiotics – live bacteria that help maintain a healthy digestive system – has grown rapidly. Of these products only a small percentage of them qualify as psychobiotics and have an impact on behavior.

What is this news about Botox for depression?

Is it really true that you can get rid of your depression and your wrinkles simultaneously? Well, in a large study from Georgetown Medical School, researchers found that more than half of their depressed patients treated with Botox showed a 50% improvement in their depression symptoms in less than 6 weeks! This study, which was published in the Journal of Psychiatric Research, included 74 patients who were injected with a single treatment of either Botox or a placebo between the eyebrows. The patients treated with Botox showed a decrease of 47% of their depressive symptoms, compared to 21% in the placebo group. Clinical Professor of Psychiatry at Georgetown, Dr. Normal E. Rosenthal, expresses his enthusiasm for the study and states "This research is groundbreaking because it offers those who suffer from depression and their doctors an entirely new approach to treating the condition, and an approach that doesn't conflict with any other treatments". He suggests that Botox may relieve depressive symptoms as a stand-alone therapy, or in combination with other treatments.

Saliva Test Reveals Teens at Risk for Depression!
A new study demonstrates that teen boys with mild symptoms of depression can be identified by taking a saliva test that predicts which of them will later develop a major depression! Researchers measured the stress hormone cortisol in teen boys. Those with high levels of cortisol and with mild depression symptoms were up to 14 times more likely to suffer clinical depression later in life than those with low or

normal cortisol levels.

The researchers tested both teen boys and girls, and found the test to be most effective with boys. About one in six people suffer from clinical depression at some point of their lives, and most mental health disorders appear before 24 years old. Currently there exists no other biological test to identify depression.

One of the researchers from University of Cambridge, Dr. Joe Herbert, explains "With this saliva test, you don't have to rely simply on what the patients tells you, but what you can measure inside the patient". Herbert and his colleagues observed more than 1800 teenagers aged 12 to 19 and examined their cortisol levels with saliva tests. The researchers also worked with the teens' reports of depression symptoms and tracked diagnoses of mental health disorders in them for up to three years later. The boys who had high cortisol levels and mild depression symptoms were up to 14 times more likely to suffer from clinical depression when compared to other teens with normal levels. Girls with similarly elevated cortisol levels were only up to four times more likely to develop the condition. Leading psychiatrists find this saliva test very promising as it can help target psychological help earlier for boys at risk of developing serious depression.

Concussions linked to depressions.

Another recent study shows that teenagers with a history of concussions are three times more likely to suffer from depression. Up to 3.8 million sports and recreation related concussions occur each year in the US making it important to be aware of the risk of depression following concussions. The study was conducted on 36.000 adolescents but it is uncertain how soon after a concussion you are in high risk of developing depression and if it is an ongoing risk for the rest of your life, or only for a short period after the concussion.

"Depression taught me the importance of compassion and hard work, and that you can overcome enormous obstacles"

(Rob Delaney)

16. IS THERE LIFE AFTER DEPRESSION?

Will I ever get better, and what will my life be like after depression? This question is one many depressed people have asked themselves while suffering a depression.

First of all, know that you can get better and you will get better, if you get help! There are so many well documented depression treatments available today and with the assistance of a professional health provider, you will also find the right treatment for you.

Major depressive disorder can be a long-term or even lifelong illness for many patients and for them a continuation therapy or maintenance therapy can prove valuable, as this is intended to prevent relapses. If you have experienced major depression and have had a remission, you are still at risk of a depressive relapse, and it is important that you continue seeking information and help to remain depression-free. About 50% of patients with chronic depression who responds well to treatment will still suffer a relapse within 1-2 years if they stop treatment.
So it is important that you ease out of your treatment with help from a healthcare professional. The duration of maintenance therapy is usually 6-24 months, but for some patients maintenance therapy is needed for an indefinite amount of time and may turn into lifelong treatment.

In general the best personal practices to follow to remain depression free include:

Limit or exclude very big stressors in your life, as ongoing psychological stressors affect our daily functioning and may lead to major depression. This is especially important to people who have previously suffered from depression.

Avoid all illegal substance use and daily or frequent alcohol intake. Substance abuse can be a big contribution factor for a depression relapse.

Practice regular and healthy sleeping habits that prevent insomnia. Become and stay physically active and fit. New research shows that moderate and regular exercise can actually prevent depression in the long term.

Meditate.

Have overall good and healthy eating habits that nurture your body and brain functions.

Nurture your relationships, have close friends to confide in and stay social.

Stay mindful in the present and don't dwell on past bad experiences.

We all have unexpected, sad and serious things happening to us during our life time, and if you have previously suffered from depression, your risk for a new depression will be higher if traumatic events happen. But on the positive side you will often also be able to recognize the symptoms of depression much earlier, and be able to change direction and seek help to prevent a full-blown depression recurrence.

Take care of your own needs, dreams and desires.

Establish a good relationship with a medical doctor and a professional health provider, such as a talk therapist who can help you maintain your remission.

Depression is cruel - there is no way around it. However, I have seen so many positive outcomes of depression also, such as people changing their whole lifestyle to the better after a depression. And I am a firm believer, that after any mental breakdown, that can be depression, stress and/or anxiety, when we come out on the other side – we come out stronger, wiser and more aware of our values and priorities in life. And all in all, that is not such a bad thing.

"Out of suffering have emerged the strongest souls;
the most massive characters are seared with scars" (Khalil Gibran)

17. SOURCES AND LINKS.

The Mayo clinic – subscribe to Managing Depression e-newsletter to stay
up to date on depression topics. http://newslettersignup.mayoclinic.com/?fn=210

The National Institute of Mental Health (NIMH)

WHO

Havard.edu

"Novel model of depression from social defeat shows restorative power of exercise"

Amen, Daniel, M.D. "Seven simple brain-promoting nutritional tips to get your diet
under control and use food as brain medicine"

PLOS Medicine Dr. Alize Ferrari

JAMA Psychiatry Dr. Rebecca Pearson

Journal of Neuroscience

"Top 10 Depression Links Debunked" by Deborah Gray

Benedict Carey "Sleep Therapy seen as an Aid for Depression"

American Journal of Public Health

Health.com

Combatting Depression with Exercise" by Shelly Scott, M.D.

Medicalnewstoday.com

Psychcentral.com

Webmd.com

Psychologytoday.com

Allaboutdepression.com

Genome.gov

Ncbi.nlm.nih.gov

www.ingramcontent.com/pod-product-compliance
Lightning Source LLC
Chambersburg PA
CBHW060835290526
45792CB00006BB/1927